For Yoko Ono and Wendell Berry
even though we've never met.

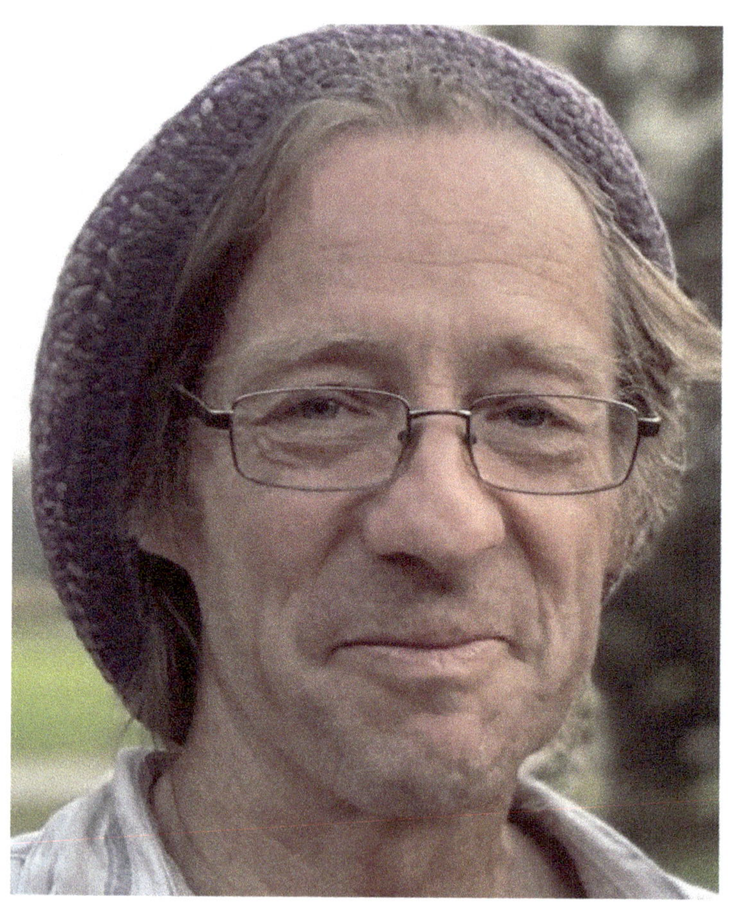

Photo of the author in 2021 (by Adeet Deshmukh).

David Bade

Five Loves and Two Wishes
Short prose and even shorter poems
1972-2022

Caimbeulach
Villa Grove
Illinois
2022

Contents

Death and Breath
(1972-1983)

En las más de las historias de la filosofía que conozco se nos presenta a los sistemas como originándose los unos de los otros, y sus autores, los filósofos, apenas aparecen sino como meros pretextos. La íntima biografía de los filósofos, de los hombres que filosofaron, ocupa un lugar secundario. Y es ella, sin embargo, esa íntima biografía, la que más cosas nos explica.

Cúmplenos decir, ante todo, que la filosofía se acuesta más a la poesía que no a la ciencia. Cuantos sistemas filosóficos se han fraguado como suprema concinación de los resultados finales de las ciencias particulares, en un período cualquiera, han tenido mucha menos consistencia y menos vida que aquellos otros que representaban el anhelo integral del espíritu de su autor.

--Miguel de Unamuno,
Del sentimiento trágico de la vida.

Almost Haiku
The moon softly shines
on a small boy kneeling
by his mother's grave
(1972)

As evening leaves us groping for yet another day

for Rich Halpern

We were sitting in a hollow room
breathing the arrogant smoke of intellectuals
rye bread
with wry laughter
and a backseat view of shallow faces
nonsense applauded
for its well-sculptured diction
I run my lazy Camel
for diversion among the ashes
We're all trying so hard

We were walking
with nothing to say
talking so fast
no time to answer
till the stranger blocked our path
and with his nebulous oration
begged us crave his mysterious secrets
made us crack
into smile
at all of us

I was standing by a mirror
leaning on myself
you were knocking on the ivories
looking like a poet
with nothing to say
hitting some of the notes

I remember you that way
always running back
for the notes you'd missed
both of us scared to be wrong

We were sitting in semi-tense silence
with everything to say
the music faded and desperate smiles dropped gaunt
as we cried out to be wrong
losing hope but wanting to believe
we hadn't seen it all
(1978 or 1979)

Touch me
i
Some days are plain
yawns and bus rides
radios record stores
typewriters and books
pushy crowds vegetarian
delis traffic signals
and conversations
Then you touch my ear
gentle as lightning
yet not as illuminating
and I turn to find
You've dissappeared.

Dissappointed, frustrated
longing to meet you again
prepared now to listen to your
touch and feel your words sink
deep into my soul
you caught me unaware
left me in turmoil
restless, straining
or shattered
for a day that won't end
till my tears fall asleep
on my hands.

Touch me

ii

At night when the moon is shining the trees cast
their long shadows over the water
the air moves the grasses softly make me want to
join them in their adulatory undulations
bending over earthward worshipping
in honor of whom I'm not certain
my restlessness abates in this sedentary
environment
my thoughts rising to catch up to my soul

Who are you who breaks into my noisy world
        calling my name?
Who are you who shines in my shadows by day?
Who are you who beckons me to follow, leaving
        only your feel and a star which smiles at me
        from so far away?
Why is it that the only times we share
        are when I am alone?
Why is it that the only times we share
        you tell me my friends are wondering where I
        am?
(1978 or1979?)

The false appearance of day
The house is empty
and the night silent
save the streetlight humming
the quiet and the dark
do not shield me
from the aftermath of day
I stand still
feel the frozen void
the streetlight humming
its passionless appeal
the false appearance of day
Alone I gather up what remains
from the numbing onslaught of day
the dogs begin their barking
instinct calling in vain
for the resurrection
I shudder from the cold
and close the door
(1978 or 1979?)

The Wind
The wind unchained
carresses
laughs
and whispers
of a million journeys
(1979-1980?)

Today I'm One
cradle the earth in my hands
kiss it till it giggles
(1979-1980?)

A period of labour
The silent smiling spaces
behind your careful eyes
hints of glories born
inside your pregnant mind
children concieved
in imagination
stolen by the Piper
while they yet lay within your womb

Whose heart returns
to a love that lies?

I've seen you in my dreams
wiped the tears from your eyes
and often in the evening quiet
I wonder when from your womb
the child of such long labour
will finally be born.
(1981)

When I was very young
I would call to birds
and animals and they would
always run away
Now that I am older and have glimpsed
the sadness of fear
I do not call them
and they wait at a distance
watching with the eye of suspicion
I think we must live long and intently
before we can bury
the sadness of fear
(1982)

Who speak with no words
An old Chinese lady
lives alone in the next room
she does not speak.
But late at night
I hear her flute
Slowly
she plays simple notes.
Children's songs.
For hours.
(1982)

Out here
the horizons go about naked
beg you to understand
they're waiting for you
(1982)

Breathing
Out here you can see
you can walk
till you know you're alive
you can stand here amazed
realize that there is no end
that this just keeps on going
as long as you breathe
And then when you are alive
when you have spread your life out
to meet those horizons
when your body is sand and rock and rain
and your spirit is the wind and the sky
and your smile is the sun
and your sleep is the moon and the stars
and your dreams are light in dark places
not dark in light places
Then you pray
You pray they don't take your breath away
(1982)

The shepherd shouts to the mountain
he calls it down
flings his words away
music
words come back on the wind
(1982)

The wind weaves a pattern in her hair
she leaves it
wears it
like a crown
(1982)

The Sun King
Good Morning
I am the Sun King
I shine on time
and not before
And after winter's ice
I bring you Warm
(1983)

Five loves and two wishes
(1983)

I

Papierosów
An old Polish man used to work with me at night.
We could never talk but we smiled and waved.
One night I gave him a can of V8; it was all I had with
me. He came later with a ruddy smile and the only
thing he could find. I got a pack of 20 genuine Polish
"Sport" cigarrettes. I smoked a few. They are stale
now. I've kept them for five years in a small bag with a
letter, a tiny silver cross, a dead friend's crucifix, a
dried rose, and a secret note from long ago.

II

Poland

A young Polish woman cleaned the library after
everyone left each night. She was not beautiful to the
casual observer, she was beautiful because I loved her.
Sometimes I would stay late to smile at her to say
Hello or Zdrastvuj (she spoke a little Russian)
Once I placed cardboard over the wastecan and a
chocolate bar on top. My friend wrote the note in
Polish:

"To the beautiful woman who works here at night"

She set the wastecan on top of my desk
on the piece of cardboard wrote THANK YOU

III

Allen
Allen spoke a Croatian variant of English and
I loved to hear him talk. He quit that town to go sell
hot dogs. He made it, drove a limousine. Years later I
saw him again in the City. He was smiling.

IV

Maya

Beside a volcanoe near Xela Daniel rode up on his
mule. A real character from Alice's Wonderland.
Broad leaves beneath his hat. A living scarecrow. At
the foot of Santa Maria we talked – talked about
Cakchiquel and Quiché, about horses and mules, about
America and Money.

> Do people make $5000 a year? I have a house I
> made it myself. I have a wife I love, I have two
> children who love me, I have 1/2 acre of
> potatoes, I have some chickens. I do not like
> the city.

Daniel stood and said it is good to hear of other people
and places. He must go. He chased his mule up the
mountain. I laughed at all the American athletes who
think they can run. I laughed at cheap production
homes, at health spas, at car repairs and egg substitute.
I wanted a one room hovel, I wanted an illiterate
Indian woman to love and impregnate, I wanted four
children who never tasted chocolate ice cream and Big
Macs, I wanted to die with cracked lips, cracked feet,
cracked hands and no teeth.

V

Five loves and two fishes
Down along the beach between Foster and Belmont
these beautiful Vietnamese men with bodies so thin
pants so tight and cigarrettes dangling they would
come with their beautiful wives and daughters and
sisters and spend hours working their nets pulling
those Lake Michigan perch. I would sit and watch
sometimes try to talk. The women would laugh at me
maybe because I looked so strange maybe because
they liked my blonde hair. Once they gave me some
fish. No educated Chicago citizen would eat out of that
lake but I did I and my Vietnamese friends. They were
good fish.

The Law came down once, took the nets from silent
fishermen, took the fish for their cats. I bled a little bit,
bled in some cosmic fashion, bled from the side, bled
from the head, drank a bitter cup of silence, watched
the vultures drive away smiling. My friends walked by
shrugged their shoulders, started back home. I knew I
would see them again. It takes 2 or 3 weeks to make a
new net they had told me; I even had the net maker's
address to get one myself but he was going to be busy.
That evening was a violent sunset, cast heavy shadows
behind my feet.

Struck dumb
(a period of silence, 1984-1994)

Pilsen

(from *Perra Loca's Terra Animata* 1995-1998)

I

Once upon a dime
she tried to stop her thought
so lovely and sublime
we hoped that she could not

She could not stop her thought
on a dollar or a dime;
for all her life I fought
she's a friend of mine

II

And with her sorrow in her heart
and her heart in her head
and her head in her hands
and her hands in her lap
out of the grown up world
into her lap she curled

III

Found me a lady
and my lady loves me
Fed my lady with pigeon feed
Donkey says bray bray
Horse says neigh neigh
Cow says moo moo
Dog says bow wow
Cat says meow meow
Sheep says baa baa
Goat says maa maa
Guinea says potrack potrack
Duck says quack quack
Turkey says gobble gobble
Hen says fiddle le fee
But every time she moves
my lady says
she loves me.

IV

Shall broken hand
mend broken heart
and brush in hand
speak love's fine art?
Speak to me in colour—
your birds like words
have nested in my heart.

V

Volo ut sitis (I)
(for Julia)

Call upon the ransomed queen
to speak above the roar
sing and dance the art of dreams
mend a world that's torn
daybreak dawnbird rise and soar
red wing light on yellow rose's thorn
crimson dawn calls morning's golden stream
for my beloved's beauty all the world's reborn

VI

Turning (Volo ut sitis II)

Gently night slips softly into light
day shades lightly into dark
out of hiding shadows appear
stretch their meanings over fear
to give the evening dreams their stark
uncertain shifting
Your silent music moves—
curls within my ear

VII

Madrugación (Volo ut sisis III)
(for Elaine)

Wing away
measure sky
earth wind and flyer
over me

Sing away
whistling wind
life light and song
over me

VIII

Origin of language

I'll speak when I am spoken to
and not before
though my hand is broke in two
my wrist still sore
I found a voice I never knew
nor heard before
comes not from me nor you
yet speaks through us and more.

Festgedichte
(2006 and 2011)

Seven prepositional poems for Roy Harris on his 75th birthday (2006)

I

In the pink

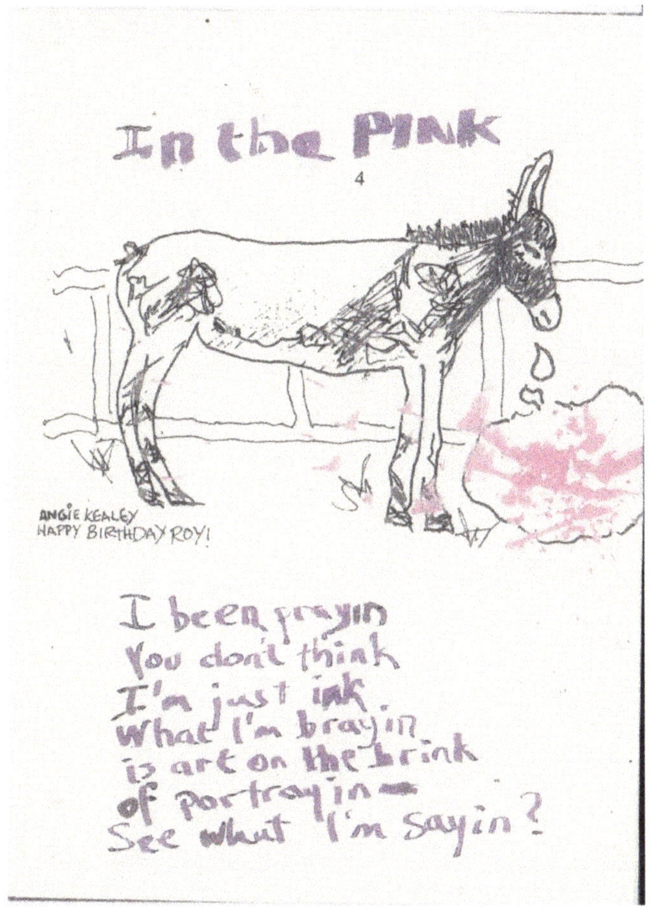

II

In the yard
The fox on the hay
No rabbit today
She seemed to say
Then went away
Hungry
In January

III

In the barn
Chain on the gate
Hay on the floor
Father is here
Opening the door
The bull is near
But the calves are late

IV

In the field
Lost my cow!
Where is she now?
Look! What do I see?
Coyote watching me!

V

In the oak tree
Robin in the oak tree
Always living free
Now up! In the sky so blue
That cat can't catch you!

VI

In the cold
January moon
So bright so white
January coon
Aren't you cold tonight?
Dawn arriving soon
My heart is light

VII

In the books
So many loves that sigh and heave
Will on the morrow cry and leave
But others speak in silent words
Bringing joys unlike the birds
And sometimes tales that make us grieve.
So often on a winter's eve
I take your books and sit and read
Till daybreak calls me to my herds

Three poems for Roy Harris at 80 (2011)

I

In a word
In the beginning
Things were not.
Then they were spoken,
And became as they ought.
And nothing was broken,
And nothing was not.
All signs and no token,
That speech that begot.
But we're *homo loquens*
And that means a lot:
We say what we mean—
And our nought means nought!

II

De profundis
Why did the slave sing?
For whom was his song?
Was anyone listening
Out under the sun?
Could he have worked
Had he not sung?
And had he not sung
What would he have done?
And had she been with him
What might they have sung?

III

After epistemology
What do you know?
Nothing I suppose—
But surely you must!
Says someone who knows.
Of love and lust,
And rain and rose;
From dawn to dust—
Who lives surely knows

Depth and Breadth
(2022)

La filosofía responde a la necesidad de formarnos una concepción unitaria y total del mundo y de la vida, y como consecuencia de esa concepción, un sentimiento que engendre una actitud íntima y hasta una acción. Pero resulta que ese sentimiento, en vez de ser consecuencia de aquella concepción, es causa de ella. Nuestra filosofía, esto es, nuestro modo de comprender o de no comprender el mundo y la vida, brota de nuestro sentimiento respecto a la vida misma. Y ésta, como todo lo afectivo, tiene raíces subconcientes, inconcientes tal vez.

--Miguel Unamuno,
Del sentimiento trágico de la vida.

In the park

I was twenty three years old with long blonde hair. I was walking down Garfield Boulevard from the elevated train station headed for the 57th Street book stores in hopes of finding a good book. He was twenty or thirty years older than me and fell in step with me as I walked through the park. He talked and laughed and talked some more. We went into Powell's Bookstore together and I headed to my usual spots; where he went I learned later: he went looking for books about Marilyn Monroe. As closing time approached (10 PM) I headed back towards the train station and he accompanied me. He kept talking about Ms. Monroe. When we got to the park he said he needed to stop and rest a minute, and would I wait for him. We sat down on a park bench along the sidewalk, just a few yards from the street. Suddenly he grabbed me by the throat with one hand and threw me down, lying on top of me and sqeezing my genitals with his other hand. He thrust his tongue into my mouth.

I fought, broke free, and ran. I was lucky; he did not follow me, nor did I collapse in an asthma attack.

For months I kept spitting convulsively. I could not get that taste out of my mouth.

On the street

I was twenty three or four years old with long blonde hair. While I was going under the overpass toward my home on the other side of Albuquerque, two men in a truck began following me, making lewd remarks. I got irritated, turned around and spoke in anger. How stupid of me! When they saw my face and heard my voice, they realized they had been harrassing a man for sex. This apparently made them really angry, for they pulled up beside me and stopped their truck, then jumped out and proceeded to beat the you know what out of me. After they left all I could think was "What if I HAD been a woman?" The question has oriented much of my thinking during the forty years since, and I've been thinking an awful lot.

In eternity

Somewhere, I do not remember where or when, I asked myself "How long have I been like this? What is it like to be sad?" Had it been weeks? Months? Years? I could not remember. All I knew was – how can I describe it? – contentment, joy, as the foundation and wellspring of the world, and I was that wellspring. I began to wonder, tried to remember how long I had been this way, but could not remember anything that was not just as this moment. I said to myself, "Have I never experienced sorrow, suffering and unhappiness? Did I not write many, many dreadful self-pitying poems in earlier years?" But try as hard as I could, I could remember no sorrow. I could not even imagine what sorrow could be: it was wholly incomprehensible. I came to the conclusion that I must have been this way forever.

And just as at that moment I could not remember when sorrow departed nor ever having been sad, nor even what sorrow was, so now I do not remember how long that feeling of living in the center of the universe continued nor when it departed.

But I will never forget my time in eternity.

Into stone

She came to visit me with a bottle of whisky not entirely full. We sat on the floor and she told me of the betrayal: her girlfriend had gotten pregnant. She wept as she told me how angry and hurt she was, how she wanted to do to her girlfriend just what her girlfriend had done to her. She wanted revenge and wanted it badly. She got up, came over and sat on my lap, her blouse unbuttoned and her lovely breasts inches from my face.

"Have I ever told you that I love you?"

The only words I had ever wanted to hear. But she was lying.

She left with nothing but her whisky sloshing around inside her, while I had turned to stone and remained that way for years.

At the party

We worked together for a charitable organization run by the Gay and Lesbian Bar Association. It was obvious—I could see it in his eyes and hear it in his voice—that he craved my company but for some reason he exercised complete restraint. Then one day he told me about his friend Carlos.

His friend, having learned that he had AIDS, threw a big party, inviting all his friends and all their friends and anyone else who wanted to have nonstop sex with as many men as they could handle. He did not tell them what his doctor had said. For two weeks they partied, consuming untold amounts of liquor and poppers and you know what else. Then Carlos abruptly announced that the party was over and sent everyone home. For two weeks neither Doug —for that was my coworker's name—nor anyone else heard from Carlos. So Doug broke into Carlos' apartment and found him more or less headless, seated at his kitchen table, with a shotgun on the floor and a note on the table. The gist of the note was this:

> Dear Friends: My doctor told me that I have AIDS.
> Thanks for the party. Carlos.

Not long after that I left San Francisco to live alone for a while in my grandmother's house in Paradise Illinois. Mark called me one day to say that Doug had died. I was unexpectedly devastated. I wept. Until then I had not realized that I had never loved anyone more.

Beside the pond

In the stillness of the wee hours of the morning I was standing alone beside a pond. A baby beaver came swimming up to the pond's edge, crawled out of the water, came towards me and began to climb up my leg. He or she then changed his or her mind, slid back down my leg, walked back to the pond, slipped in and swam off. I was in heaven and I knew it.

Below the barn floor

Walking alone and in silence I came into the barn and headed towards the hay mow. As I turned round the corner I saw four or five kits running and jumping and playing on the barn floor. I stood there enchanted till they saw me, and being even more surprised than I was, they all ran straight to the entrance of their den beneath the barn floor and dove in. My life has never been the same since.

Amidst the thorns

Coming out of the cow pasture through a wooded hollow on my way to the sheep paddock I glimpsed a small black creature scampering into the fork of a massive honey locust tree (my maternal grandfather William McKinley Campbell loved those trees and so do I). I walked quietly up to the tree and peered around it into the fork. A mink sat there amidst the foot long thorns, looking at me. We had seen each other before but had not previously stayed to visit. We remained there motionless, looking at each other for a minute or two till I decided that I had better get back to work. I said "Thank you" and moved on, slowly, but deliriously happy.

On that day

In my youth I read a short piece written by Yoko Ono
for the New York Times which she had reprinted as
the liner notes on one of her amazing Plastic Ono Band
record albums. She wrote: "The odds of not meeting in
this life are so great that every meeting is like a
miracle. It is a wonder that we don't make love to
every single person we meet." The Gospel according to
Yoko Ono. Reading her words, the life of Jesus finally
made sense to me. Eternal life is here and now or not at
all.

Yet everything depends on what you mean by "making
love"; when you find someone on top of you, it isn't
always love. Had I understood Yoko in a certain
manner and acted accordingly, within hours I would
have found myself in jail on charges of sexual
harrassment —if not attempted rape—and justly so.

I tell my daughter: Someday, before I die, on that day,
may I find myself in love with everyone I meet; isn't
that the only appropriate response to another creature?
For the depth and breadth of it is that none of us can
live without the love that comes from the bottom of
our hearts and spreads out to the ends of the world. Not
only towards the moon, the wind, the honey locust
trees, the foxes, the beavers, and the minks, but
towards old men in the park, young men in their
pickups and drunken lesbians in anguish as well.

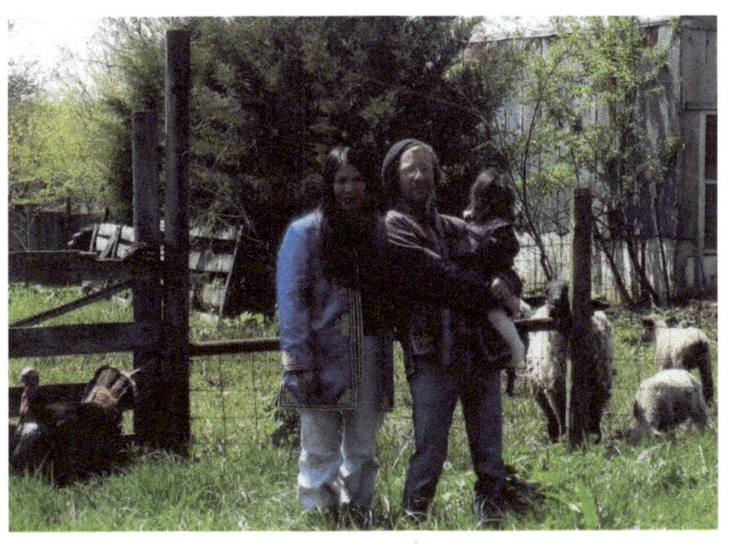

Purevbadam, David, Khaliun Rachel and friends in 2009
Photograph by Mary Margaret Bade

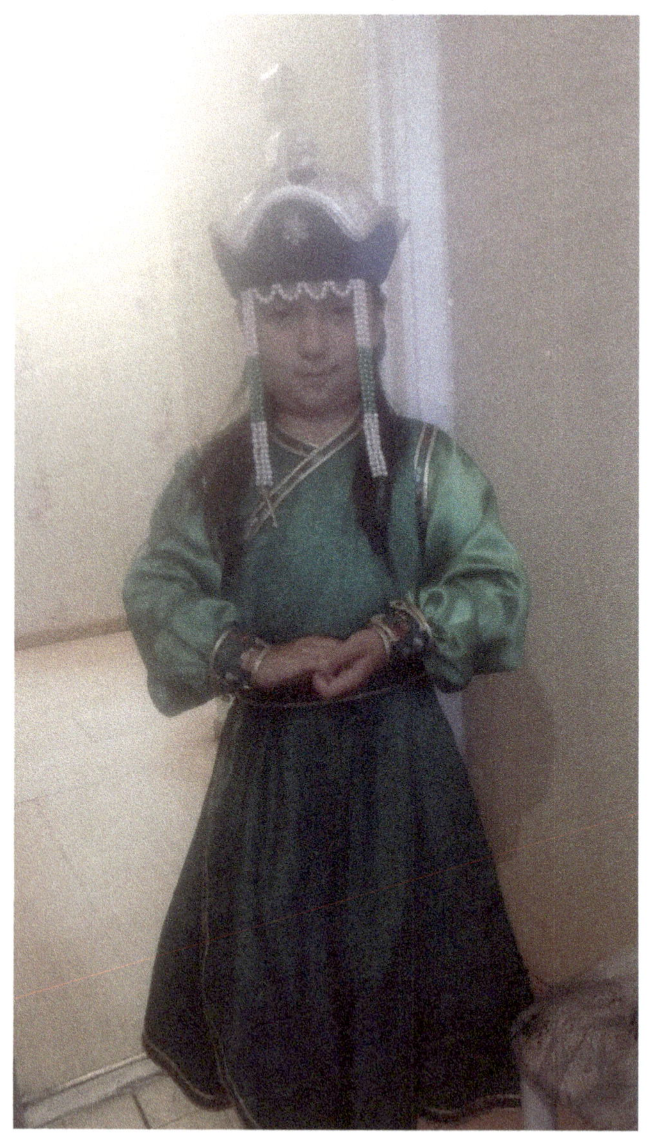

Rachel's Farm

is ninety five acres of poor grade farmland, pasture and riverbottom woodland in a floodplain, stretching from the intersection of the Champaign-Douglas County Line Road and Douglas County Road 1700E south to the Jordan Slough, and then along the Jordan's northern bank first southward, then westward to Villa Grove Cemetery and Illinois State Route 130. My grandfather (Herman Oscar Bade, 1901-1983) purchased it in a few tracts over the course of his life, passing it on to his sons. My father (Philip Ernest Bade 1929-2020) then bought his brothers' shares and from him my mother inherited it. I spent much of my childhood on the southern bank of the Jordan (when not *in* the Jordan) where I lived with my parents in what was earlier my father's maternal grandparents' five acre berry farm and is now my mother's home. The Jordan Slough runs into the Embarras River (so called, they say, because it shows its bottom in summer) where Rachel's Farm ends (on the west bank) and where my paternal grandparents' had their home for most of their life together (on the east bank of the Jordan). My father spent his entire life in Villa Grove, working with his father and brothers till his father's death, then with his brothers until they were all gone, and at the end with his son David, who spent much of his life longing to smell the manure and the hay, to return to roaming the river bottom and the pasture. I am now back where I belong, but the future belongs to Khaliun Rachel.

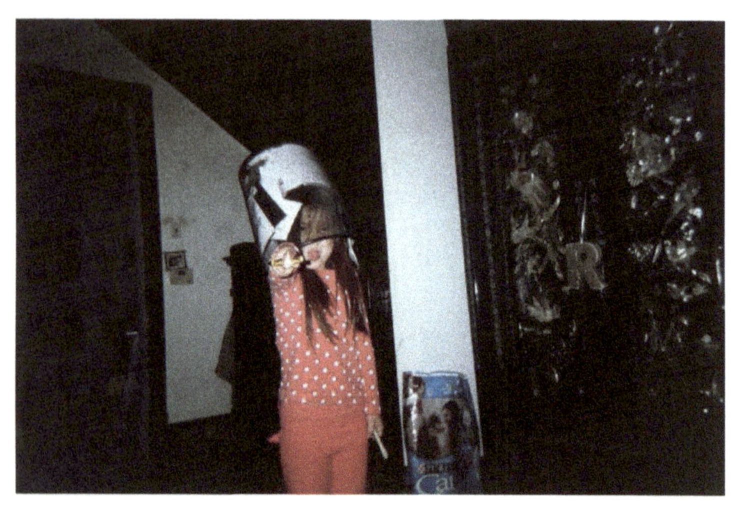

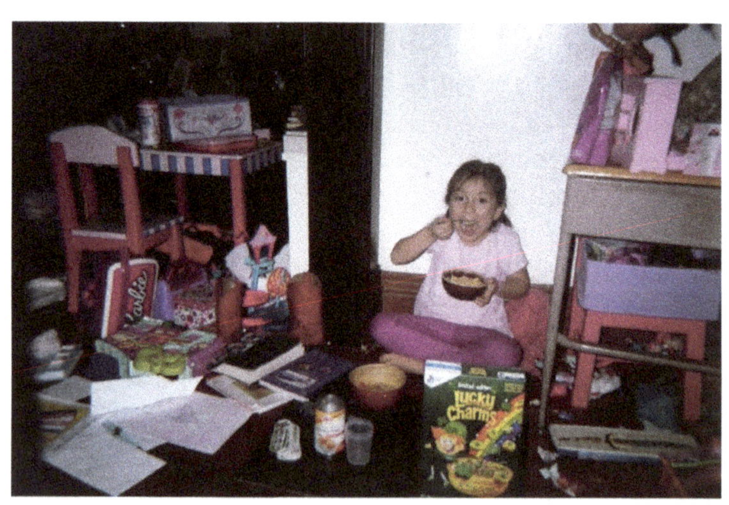

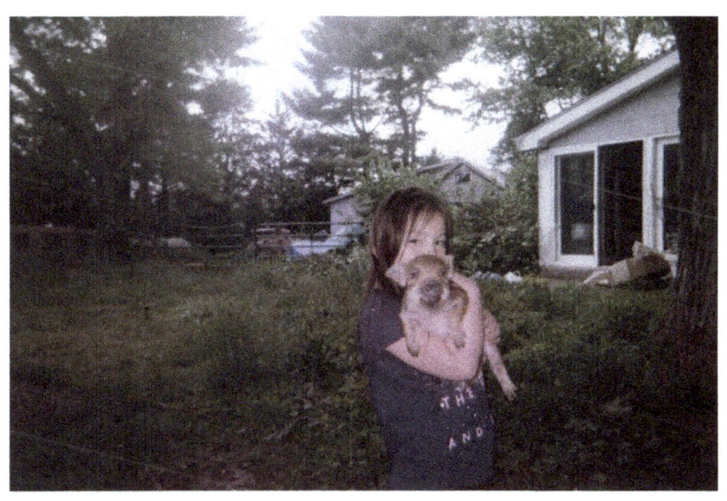

"All my life I've wanted a pig!" she squealed at 8 years old.

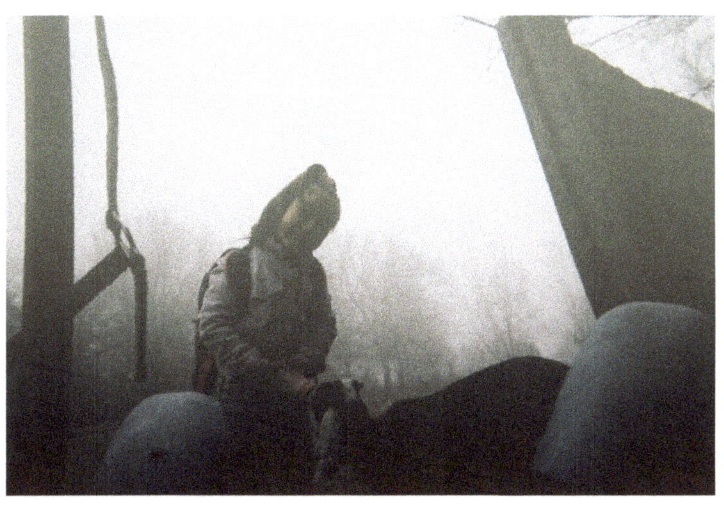

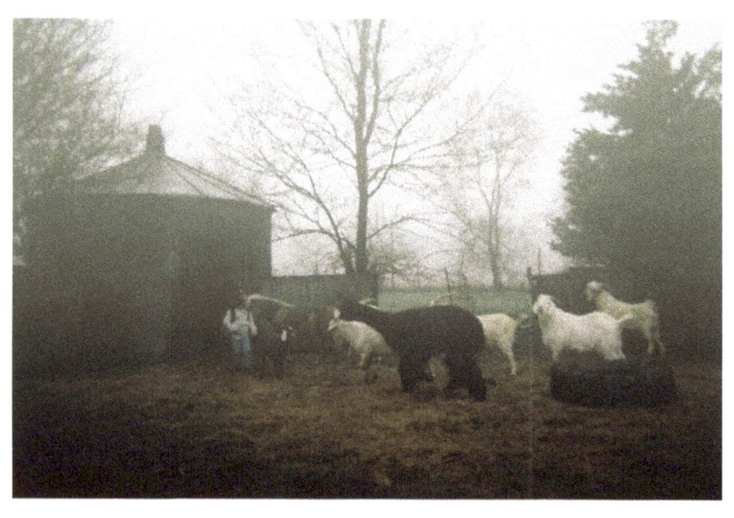

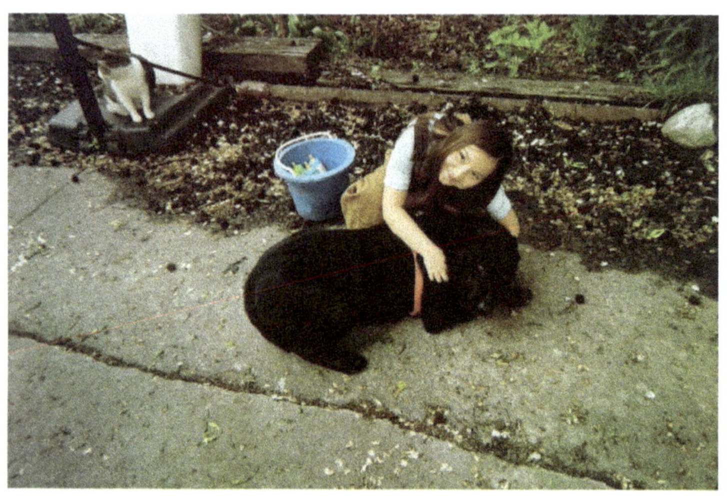

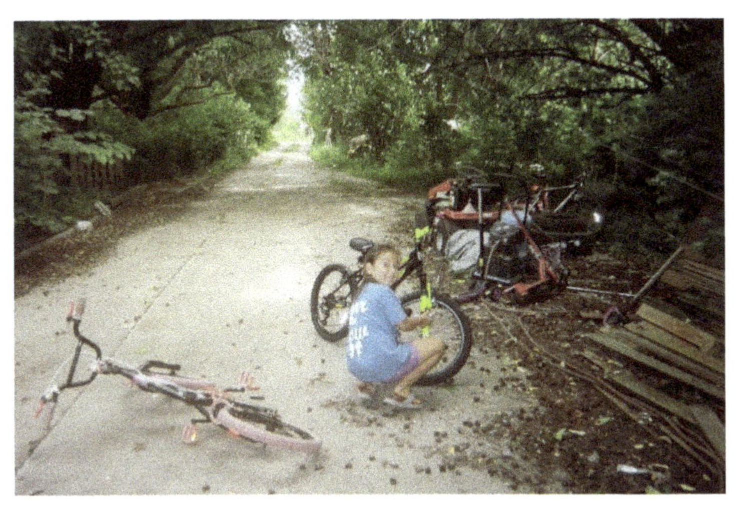

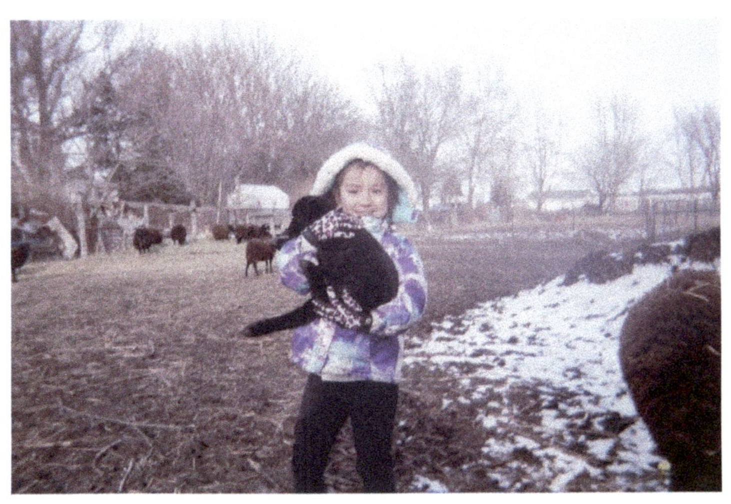

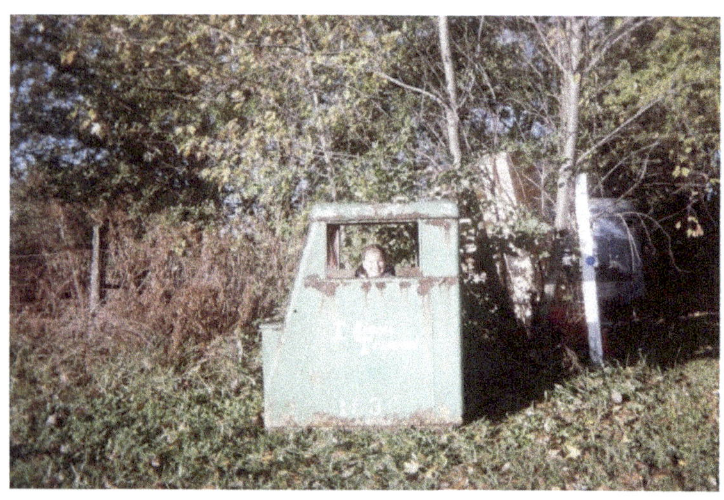

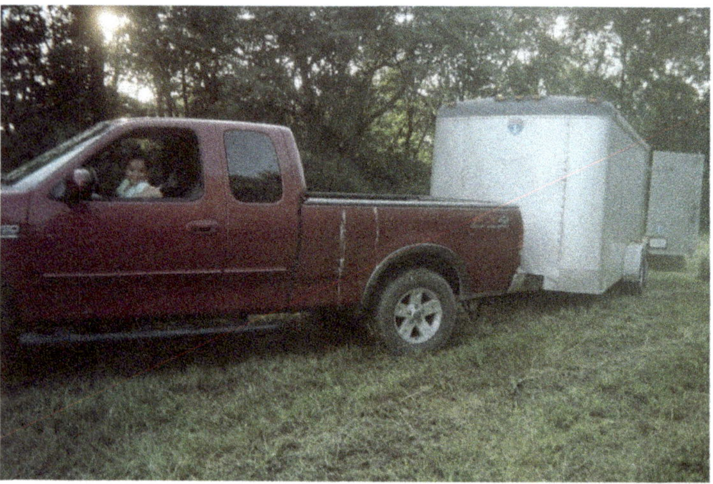

An excellent driver at 9, while I load hay in the trailer.

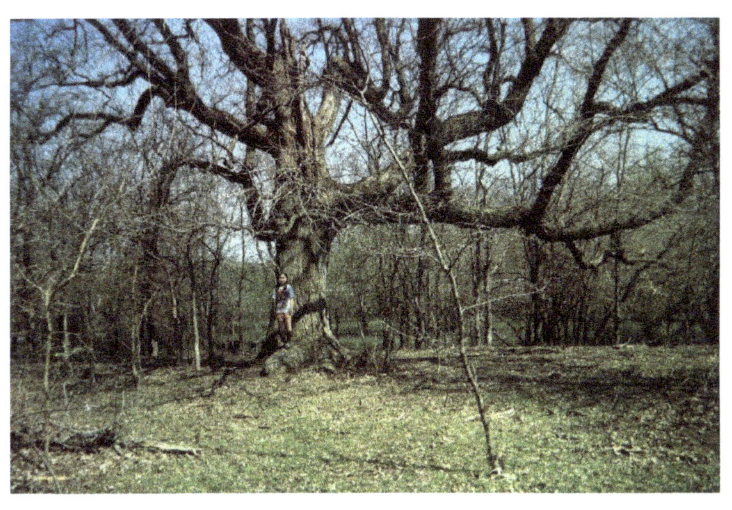

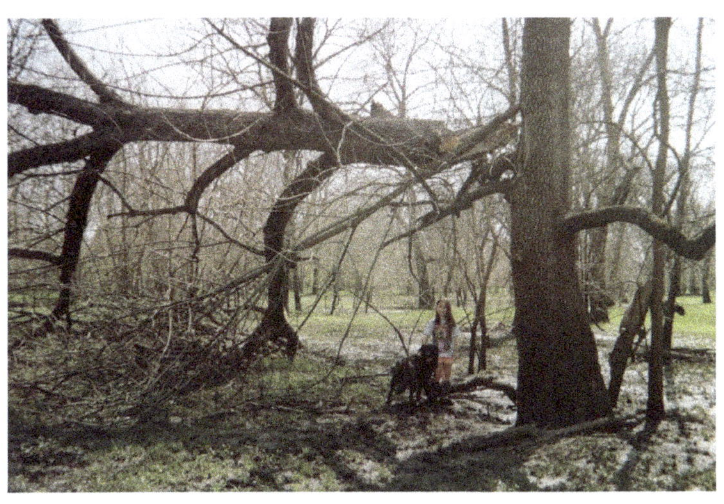

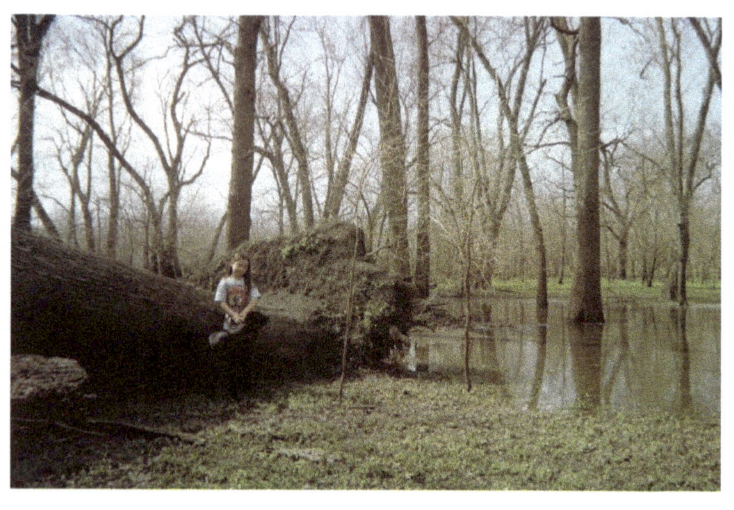

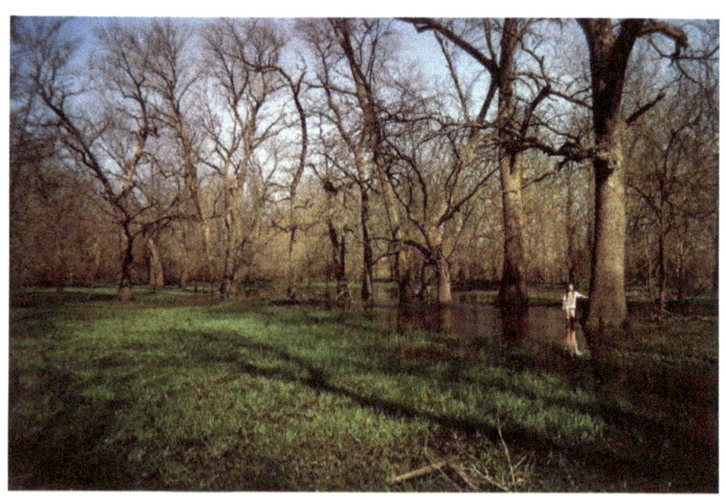

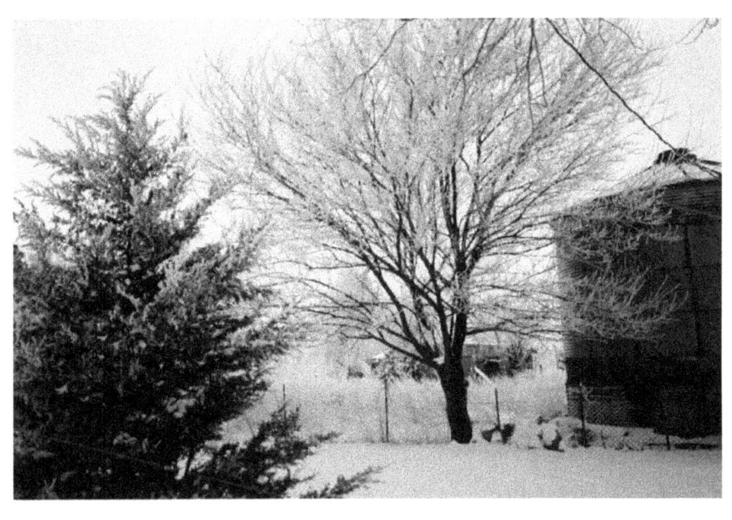

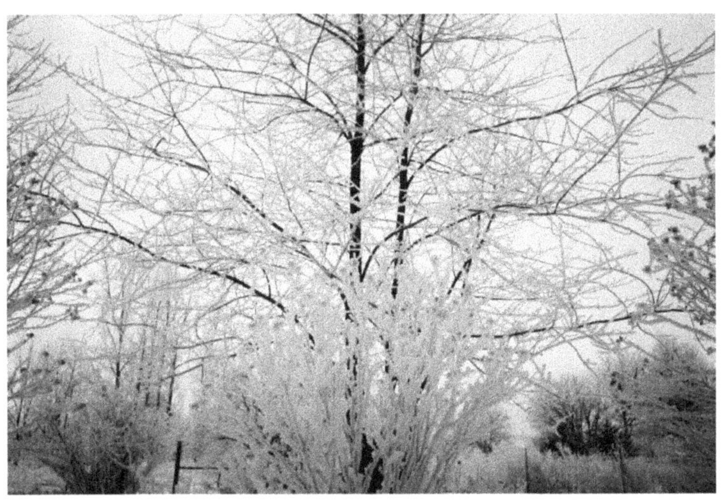

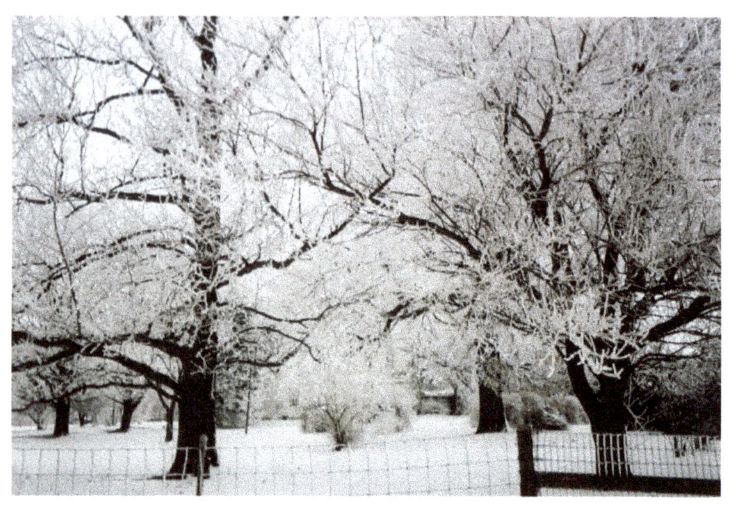

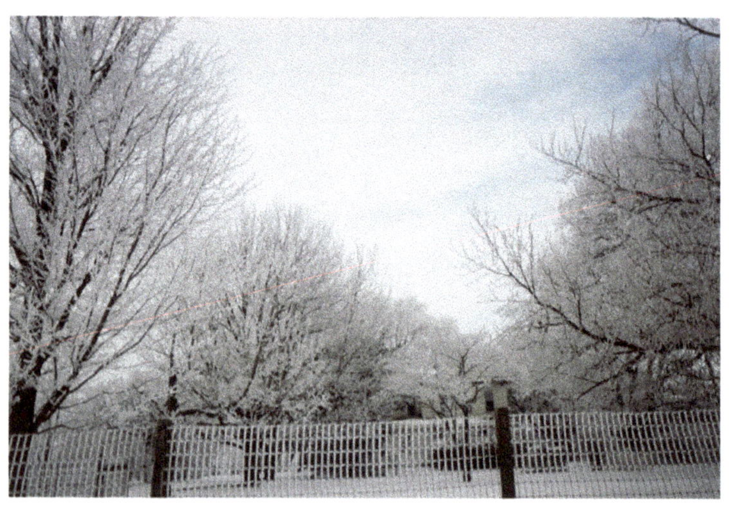

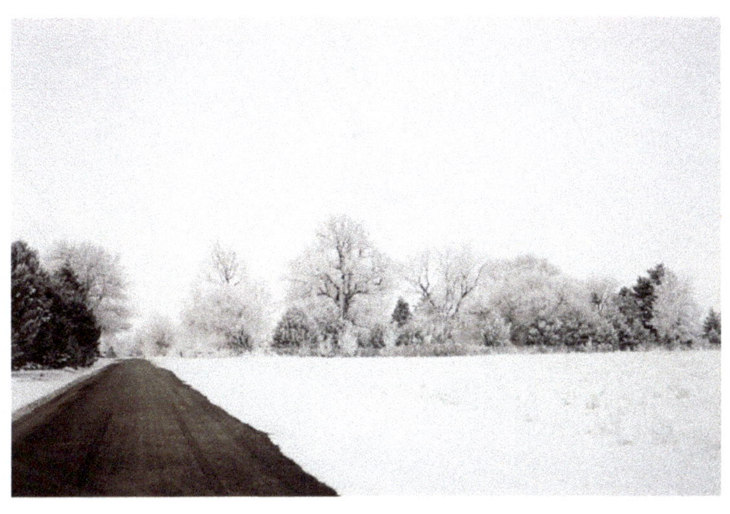

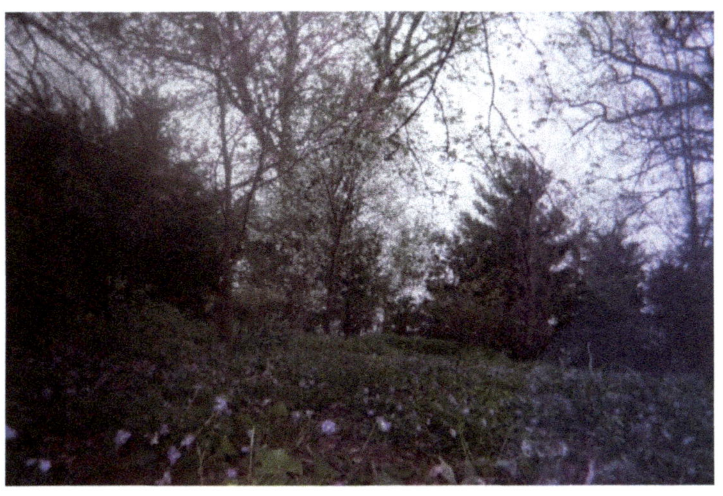

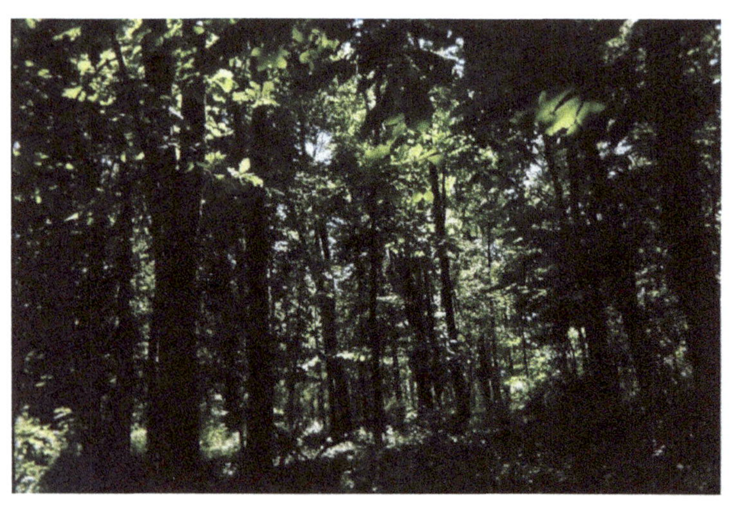

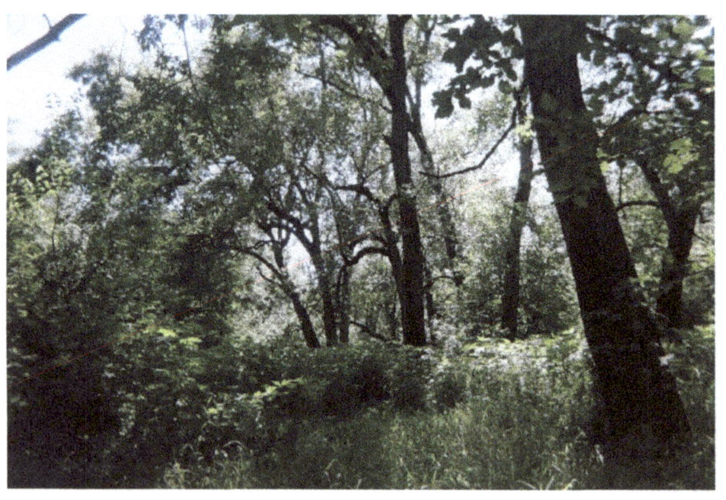

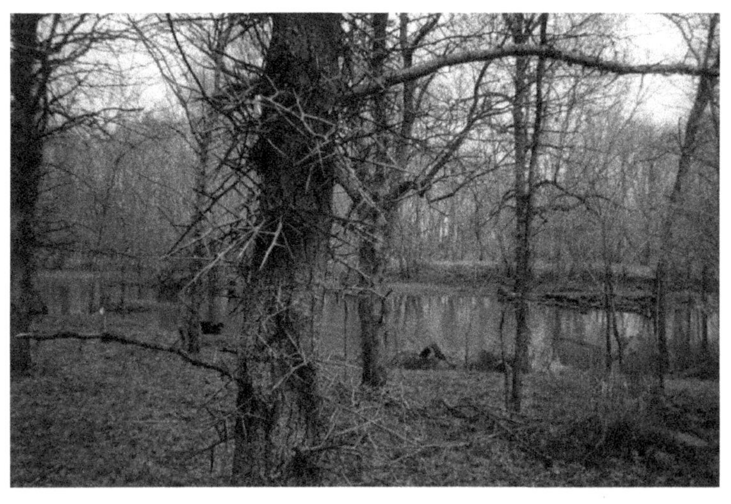

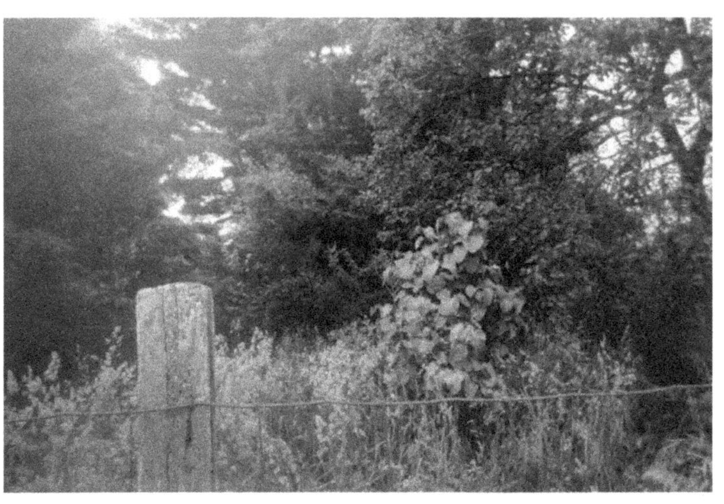

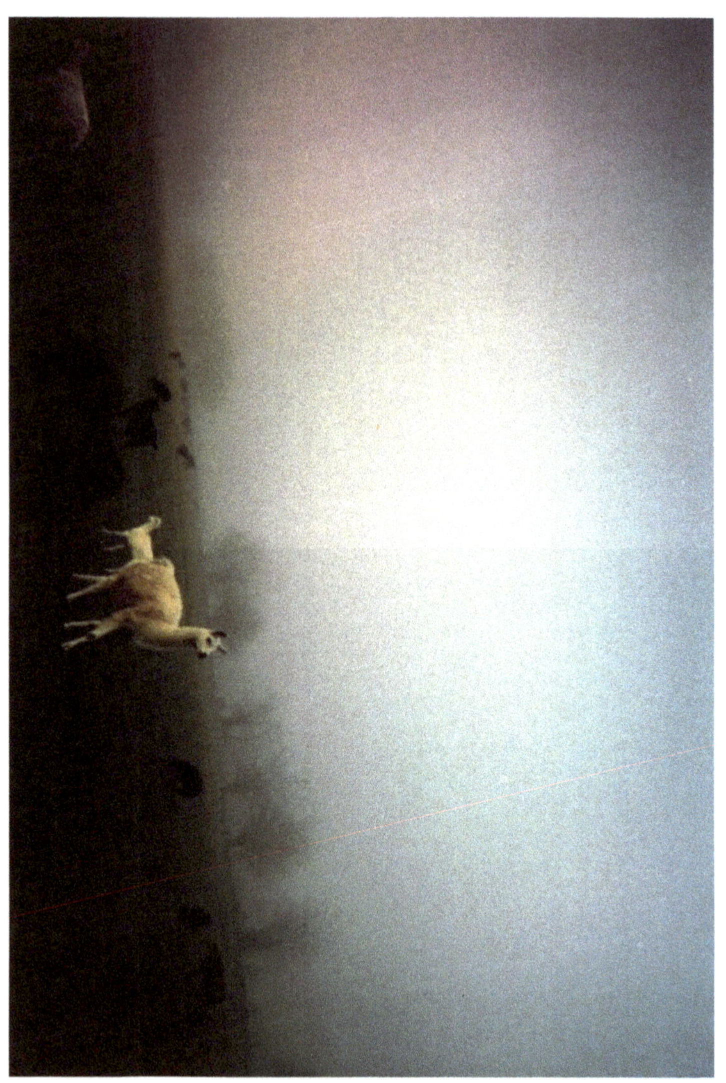

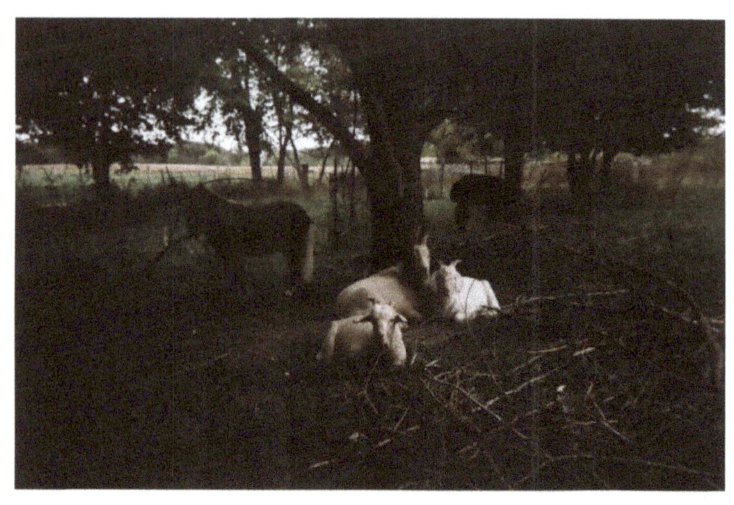

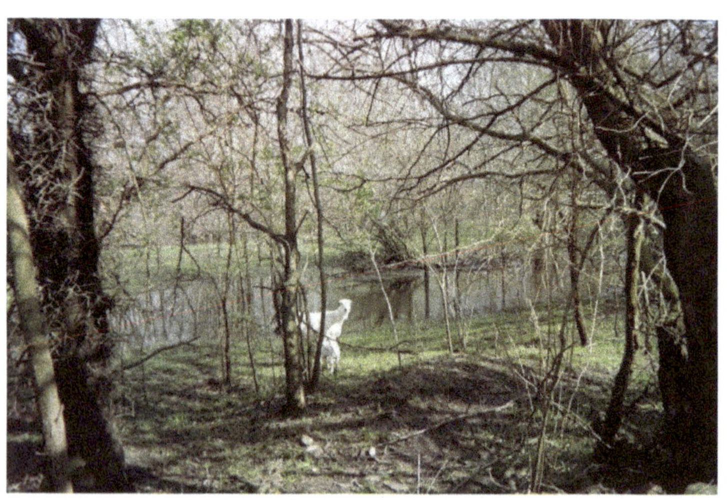

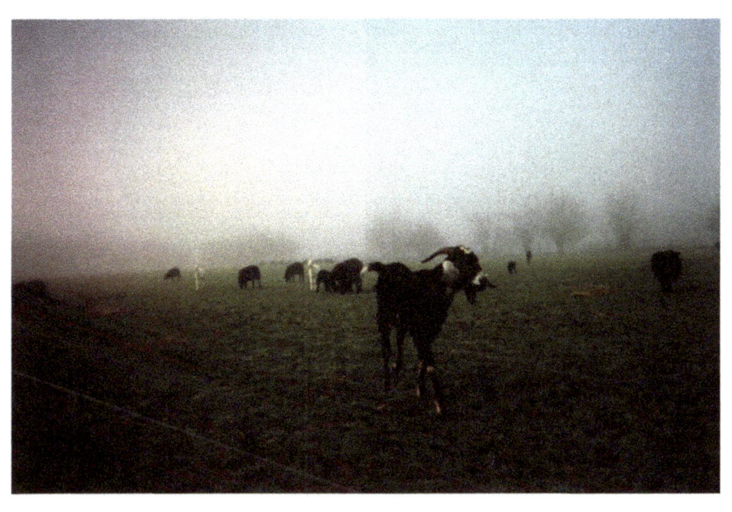

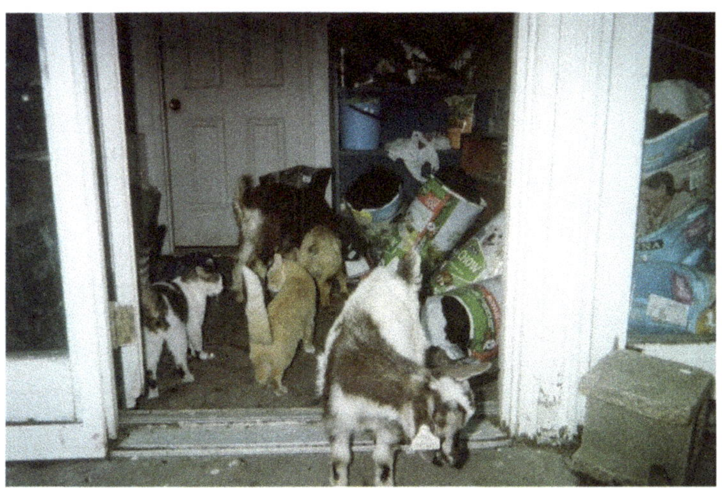

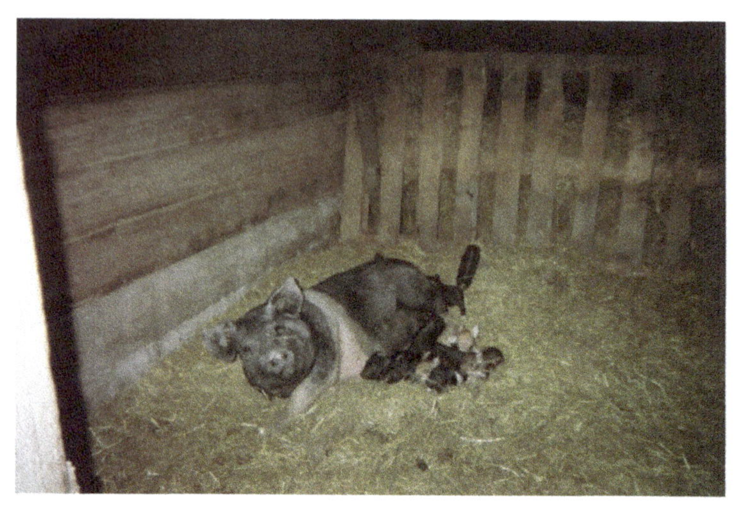

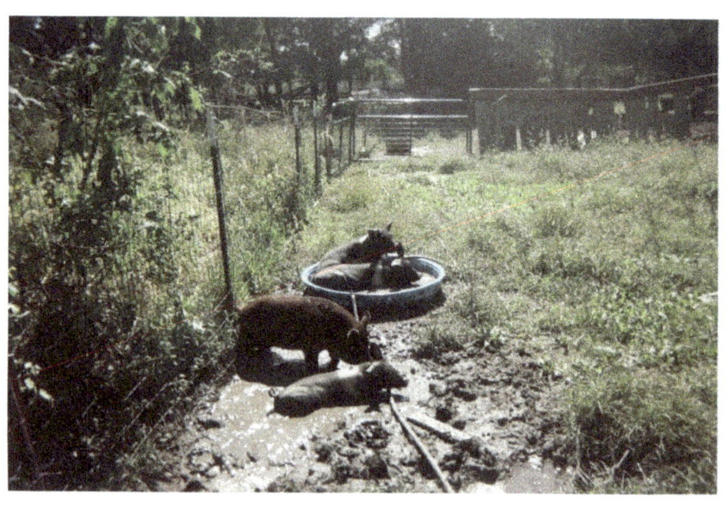

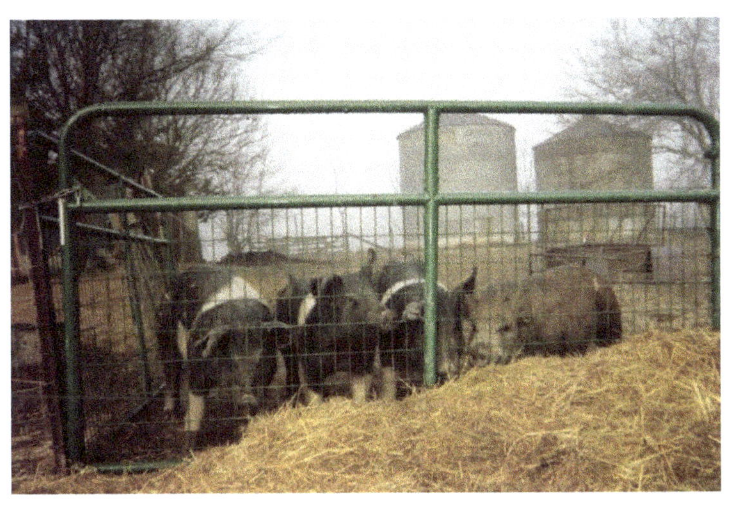

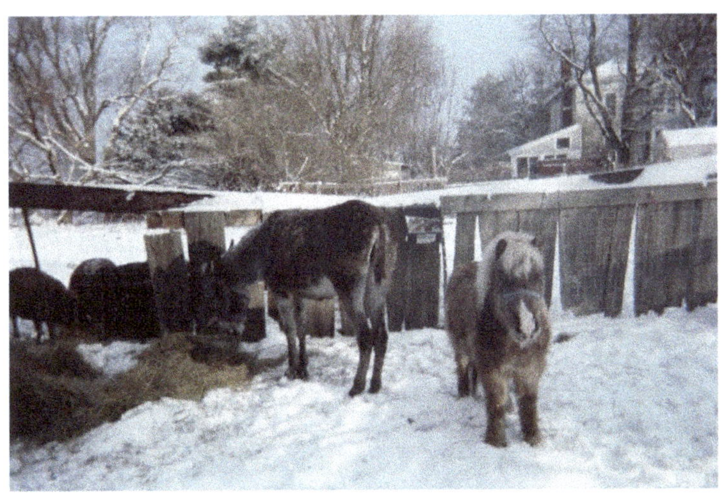

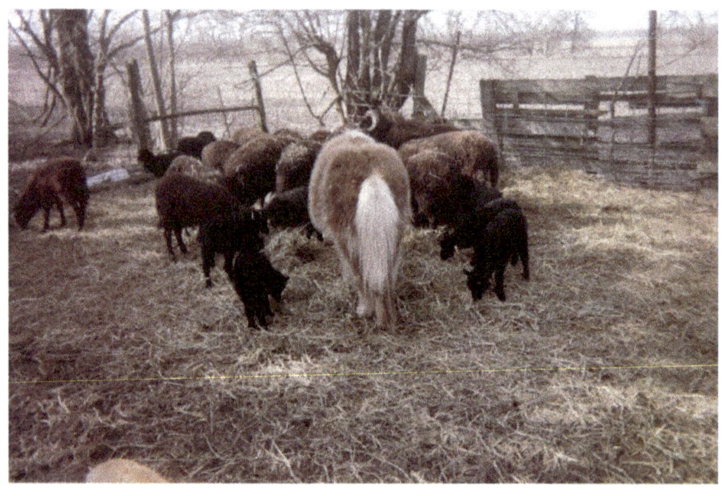

Below: Clipperd with Max Yeh's *Stolen Oranges* (Abraham in the background). What are your horses reading?

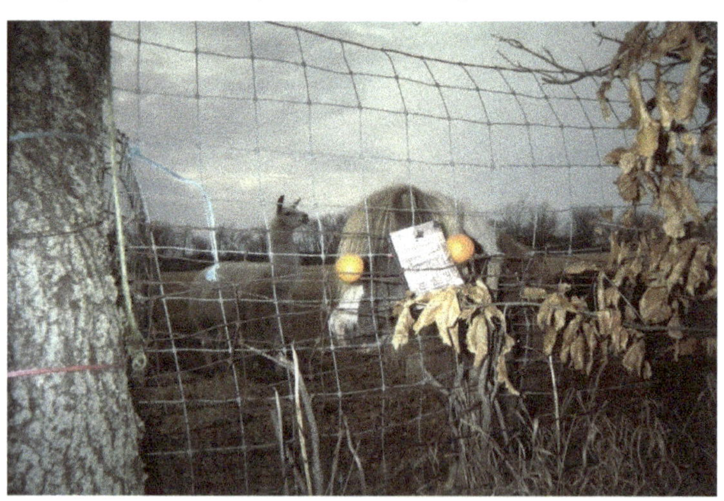

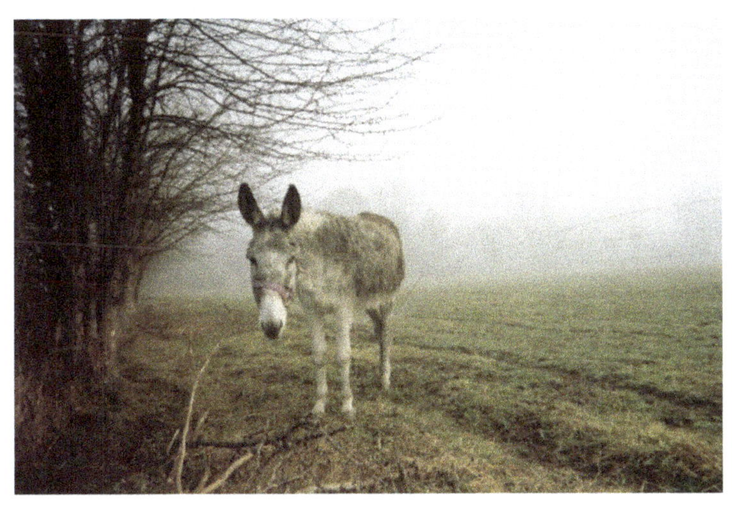

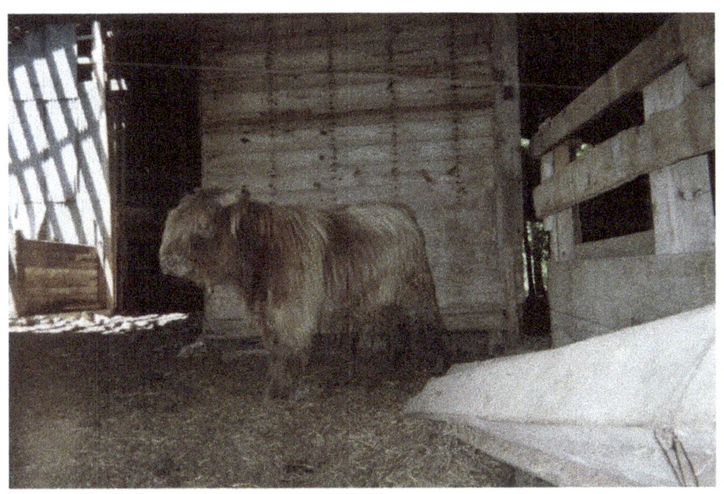

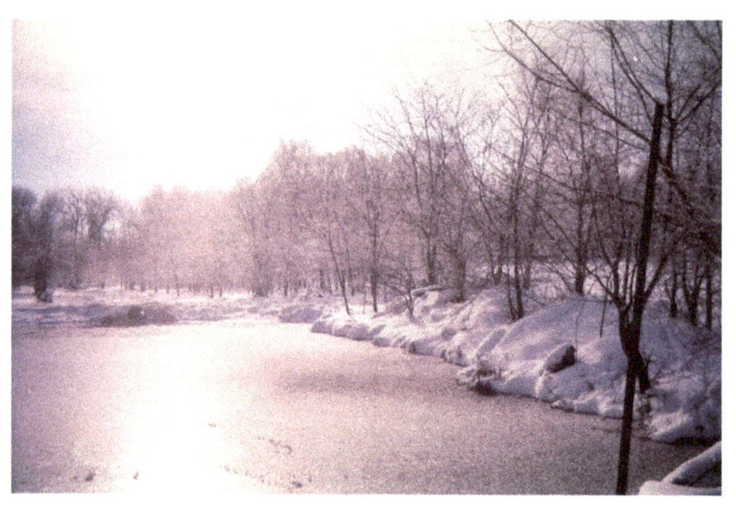

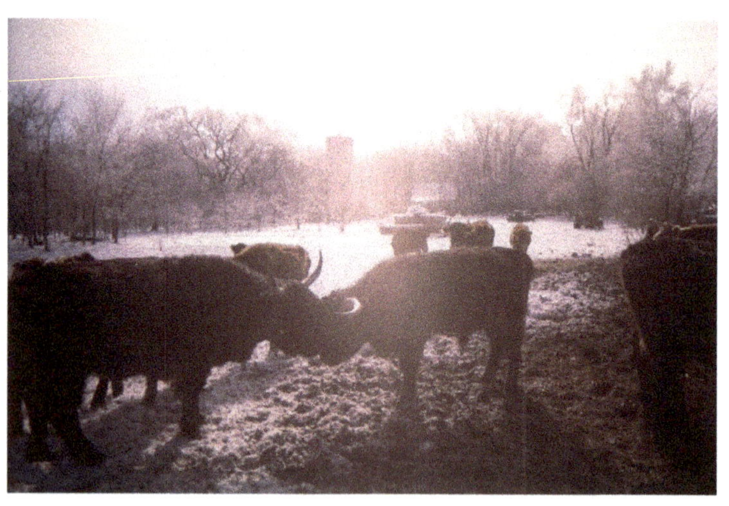

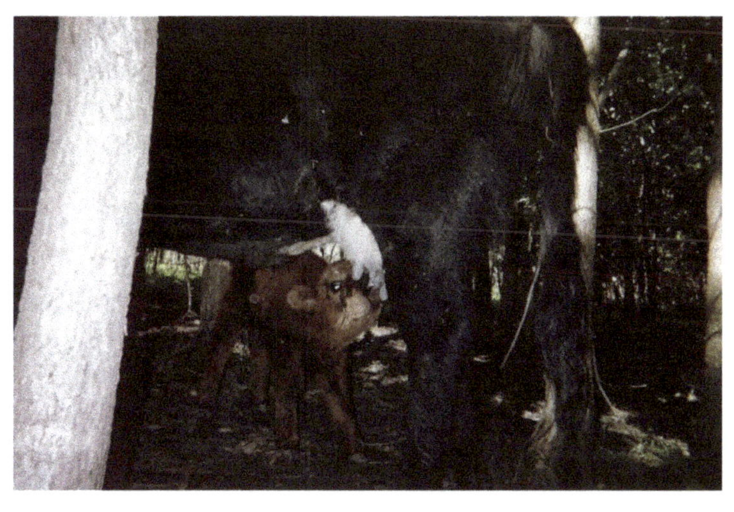

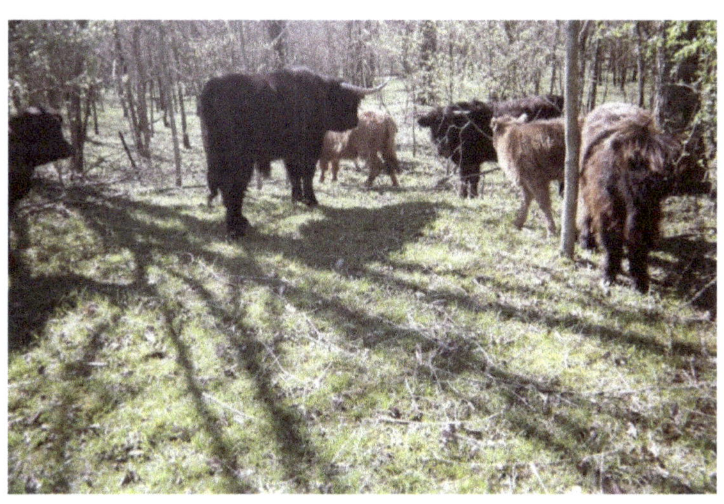

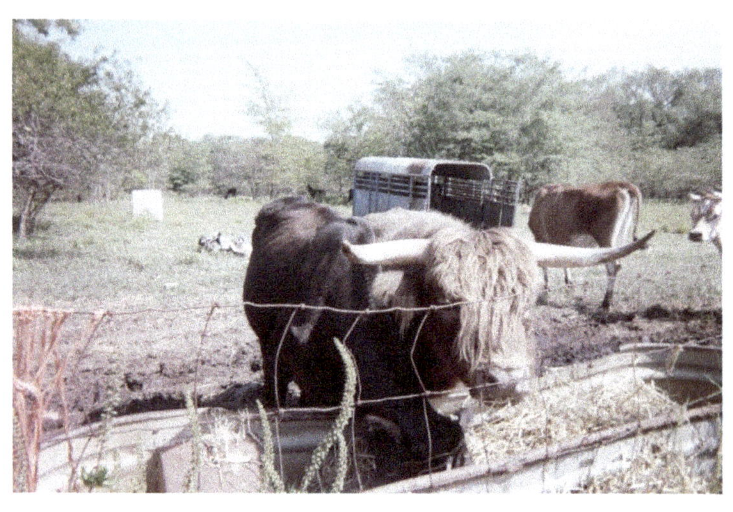

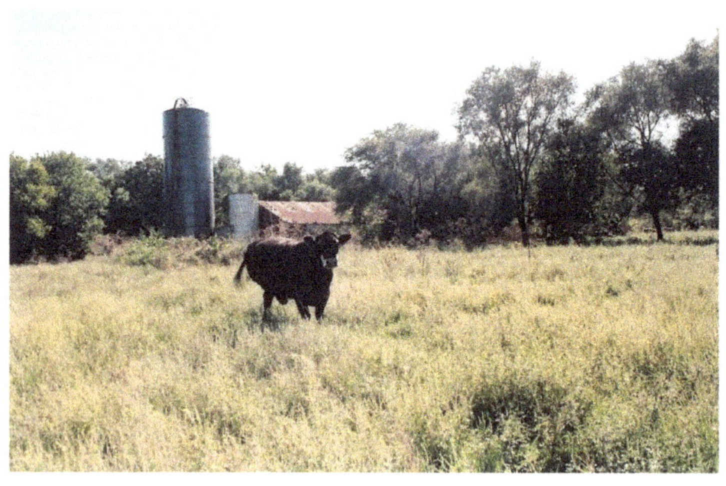

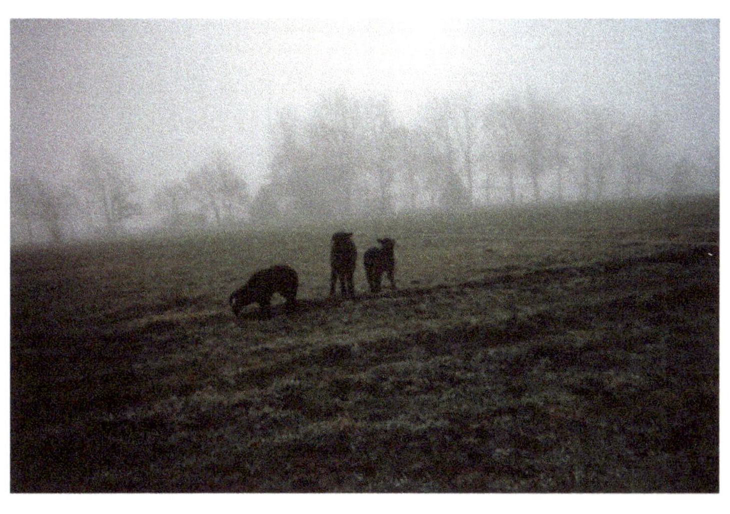

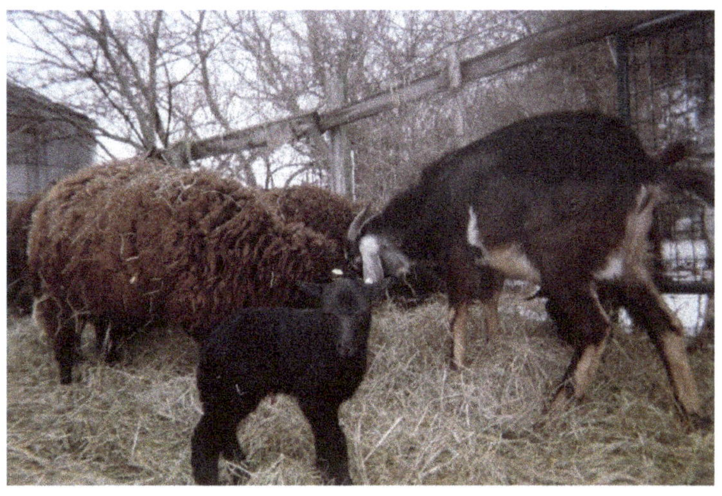

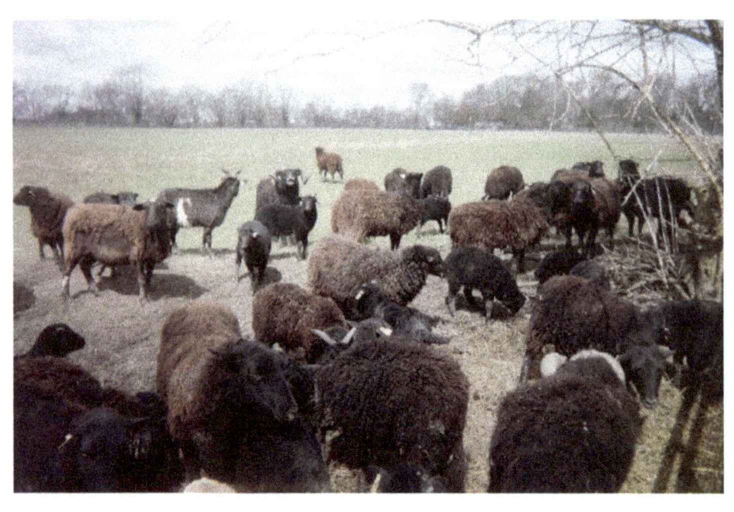

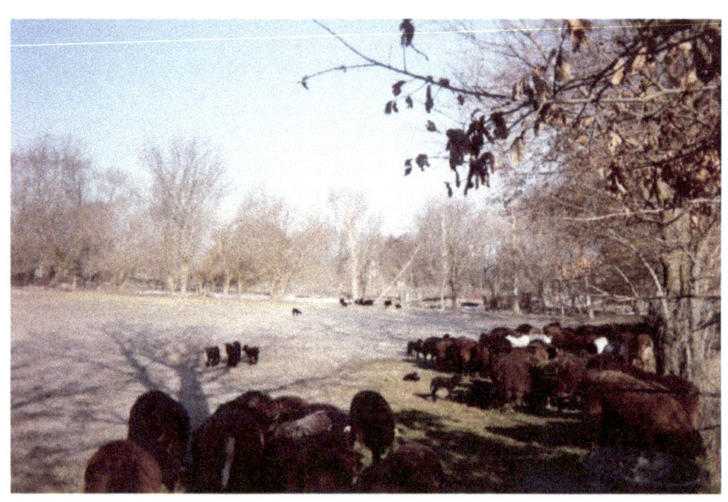

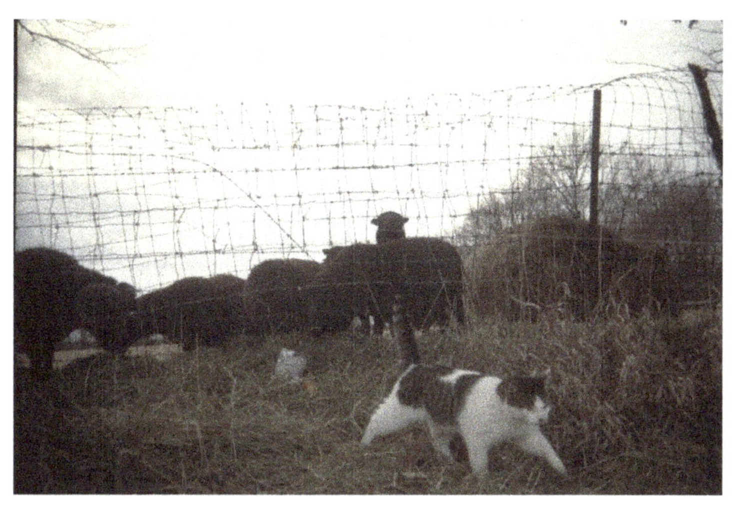

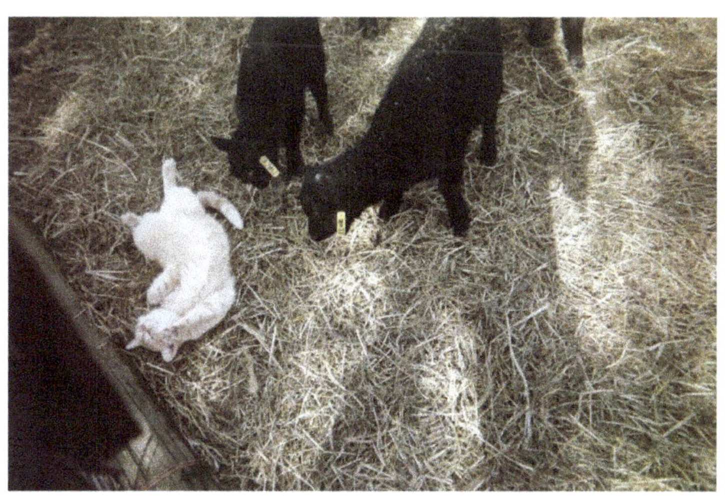

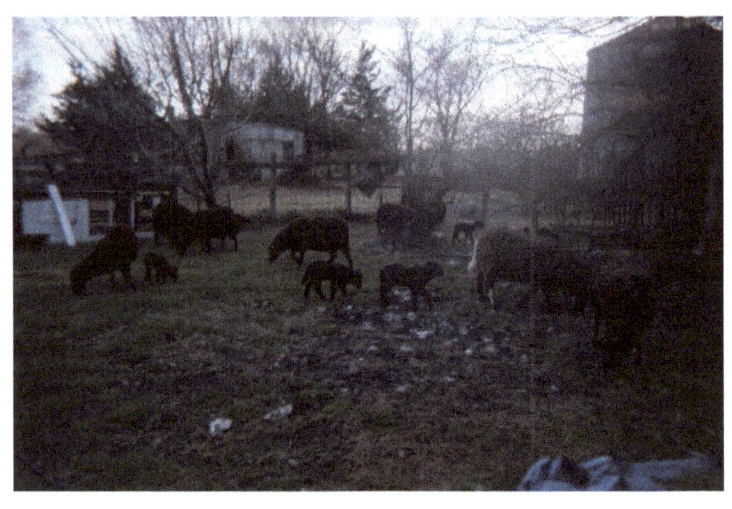

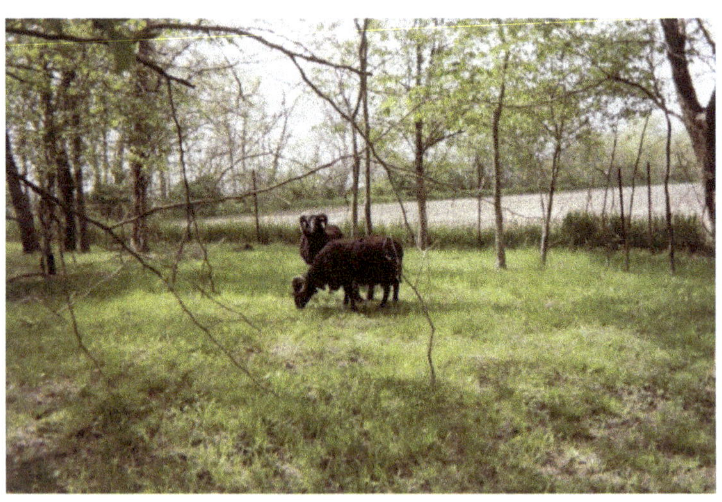

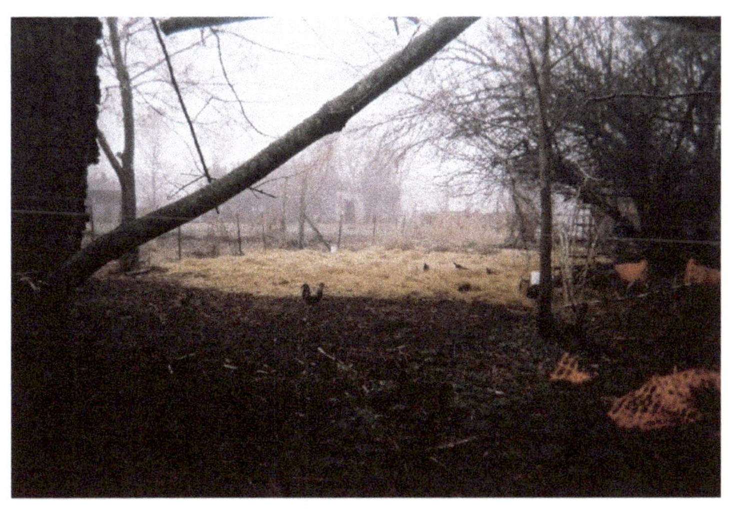

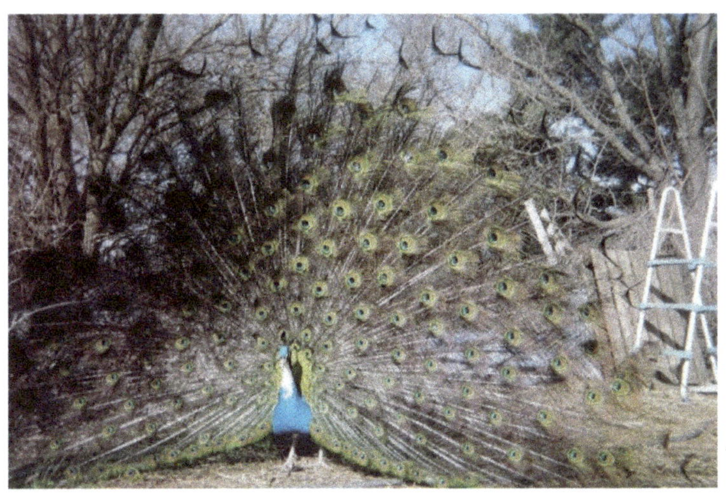

Recommended reading

ARENDT Hannah. *Love and Saint Augustine.*
BARFIELD Owen. *Poetic Diction.*
BERDYAEV Nikolai. *Slavery and Freedom.*
BERRY Wendell. *The Unsettling of America.*
BLACK ELK. *Black Elk Speaks.*
BLAKE William. *Songs of Innocence and Experience.*
BUBER Martin. *I and Thou.*
BULGAKOV Sergei. *Philosophy of Economy.*
CHARBONNEAU Bernard. *Nuit et jour.*
CIESZKOWSKI August Dołęga. *The Desire of All Nations.*
COLLINGWOOD R.G. *An Essay on Philosophical Method.*
COLLINS Cecil. *The Vision of the Fool.*
CRISTAUDO Wayne. *Power, Love and Evil.*
ELLUL Jacques. *Théologie et technique.*
FRY Christopher. *The Lady's Not For Burning.*
GASCOYNE David. *Collected Poems.*
HARRIS Roy. *The Language Makers.*
ILLICH Ivan. *Tools for Conviviality.*
INGOLD Tim. *The Life of Lines.*
KANGAS Nancy (author/editor). *Nancy's Magazine.*
KOLAKOWSKI Leszek. *The Presence of Myth.*
O'CONNOR Flannery. *Complete Stories.*
ONO Yoko. *Grapefruit.*
PAREYSON Luigi. *Ontologia della libertà.*
RAINE Kathleen. *Autobiographies.*
RONZE Bernard. *L'homme de quantité.*
ROSENSTOCK-HUESSY Eugen. *Out of Revolution.*
RUSKIN John. *Unto This Last.*
SOLOVYOV Vladimir. *The Meaning of Love.*
STEINER George. *Real Presences.*
STENGERS Isabelle. *Cosmopolitics.*
WEIL Simone. *Gravity and Grace.*
YEH Max. *Stolen Oranges.*
ZIZIOULAS John. *Being as Communion.*

Not recommended reading, being other books by the author, most of which will probably bore you to tears

Polsko-Mongolska Polka: bibliografia prac polaków oraz prac wydanych w polsce (1992)

Ještě jedna Československá bibliografie Mongolska (1997)

Books in African Languages in the Melville J. Herskovits Library of African Studies, Northwestern University: a Catalog (2000)

The Creation and Persistence of Misinformation in Shared Library Catalogs (2002)

Khubilai Khan and the Beautiful Princess of Tumapel: The Mongols Between History and Literature in Jawa (2002)

Misinformation and Meaning in Library Catalogs (2003)

Books in African Languages : Recent Acquisitions 1999-2000, Melville J. Herskovits Library of African Studies, Northwestern University, with addenda to the previously published catalog (2004)

The Theory and Practice of Bibliographic Failure, or, Misinformation in the Information Society (2004)

Perra Loca's Terra Animata (2006)

Responsible Librarianship: Library Policies for Unreliable Systems (2008)

Of Palm Wine, Women and War: The Mongolian Naval Expedition to Java in the 13th Century (2013)

Roy Harris and Integrational Semiology 1956-2015: a Bibliography (2015)

Integrational Linguistics for Library and Information Science: Linguistics, Philosophy, Rhetoric and Technology (2020)

Efficiencies and Deficiencies: Cataloging and Communication in Librares (2020)

Making Mongolians: Linguistics, Historiography, Fiction (2020)

Epistemologies of Rape and Revelation (2021)